opqrstuvwxyz

First published 1984 by
Walker Books Ltd
184-192 Drummond Street
London NW1 3HP

© 1984 John Burningham

First printed 1984
Printed and bound by
L.E.G.O., Vicenza, Italy

British Library Cataloguing in Publication Data
Burningham, John
Wobble pop.——(John Burningham's first words)
I. Title   II. Series
823'.914 [J]   PZ7

ISBN 0-7445-0168-7

wobble pop

John Burningham

WALKER BOOKS
LONDON

drip

scrub

bump

wipe

squeeze

wobble

pop

bubble

ring

abcdefghijklmn